W9-BWC-729

IS THIS NOTE FOR REAL?

Dear Ms. Carter,
Diane had the stomach flew on Friday. She'll need to take a makeup algebra test today.
Sincerly,
Ms. Webber

EVIDENCE EVIDENCE EVIDENCE EVIDENCE EVIDENCE EVIDENCE

EVIDENCE EVIDENCE EVIDENCE EVIDENCE

NO!

This isn't Ms. Webber's usual note paper.

Dear Ms. Carter,
Diane had the stomach flew on Friday. She'll need to take a makeup algebra test today.
Sincerly,
Ms. Webber

Spelling errors!

Plus, Diane's mom usually signs her name "Ms. Doris Webber."

Book design Red Herring Design/NYC

Library of Congress Cataloging-in-Publication Data
Webber, Diane, 1968–
Do you read me? : famous cases solved by handwriting analysis! / by Diane Webber.
p. cm. — (24/7 : science behind the scenes)
Includes bibliographical references.
ISBN-13: 978-0-531-12066-8 (lib. bdg.) 978-0-531-15456-4 (pbk.)
ISBN-10: 0-531-12066-X (lib. bdg.) 0-531-15456-4 (pbk.)
1. Writing—Identification—Juvenile literature. 2. Graphology—Juvenile literature. I. Title. II. Title: Do U read me? III. Series.
HV8074.W43 2007
363.25'65–dc22 2006006797

1 2 3 4 5 6 7 8 9 10 R 16 15 14 13 12 11 10 09 08 07

This is a note Diane brought from home a few weeks earlier.

From the Desk of Doris Webber

Dear Ms. Carter,
Please excuse Diane's absence on Wednesday.
She had a dentist's appointment.
Thank you,
Ms. Doris Webber

DO YOU READ ME?

Famous Cases Solved by Handwriting Analysis!

Diane Webber

Note the differences:
* Different paper
* No spelling errors
* Different signature

WARNING: This book is about some pretty nasty thieves. These people were willing to lie, cheat, and commit serious crimes to get rich. What's more, some of them had pretty bad handwriting!

Franklin Watts®
A Division of Scholastic Inc.
New York • Toronto • London • Auckland • Sydney
Mexico City • New Delhi • Hong Kong
Danbury, Connecticut

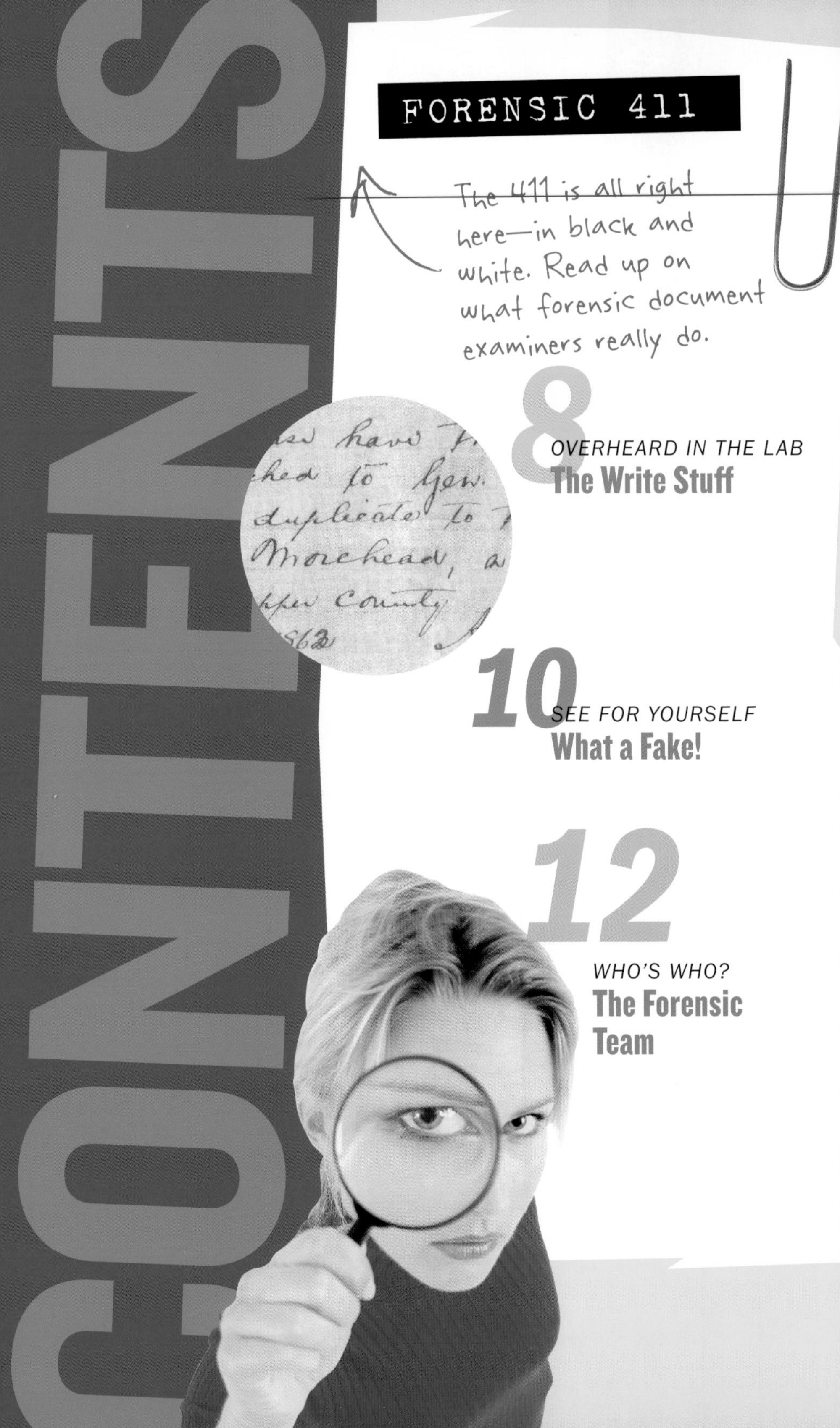

CONTENTS

FORENSIC 411

TRUE-LIFE CASE FILES!

These cases are 100% real. Find out how forensic document examiners read between the lines to solve these mysteries.

The son of Charles and Anne Lindbergh is missing!

15 Case #1:

The Lindbergh Kidnapping

It was a crime that shocked the world. Could handwriting analysis crack the case?

27 Case #2:

The Grandmother, the Will, and the Brand-New Porsche

Phyllis Davis died and left a fortune to her grandchildren. But who actually signed her will?

Has a will been forged in Canterbury, England?

Did this evil dictator keep a diary?

35 Case #3:

The Case of the Hitler Diaries

The German dictator terrorized the world. More than 35 years later, a collector produced 40 notebooks. Were they really Hitler's diaries?

FORENSIC DOWNLOAD

Are you writing all this down? Here's even more information about forensic document examiners.

YELLOW PAGES

Some criminals create evidence with the stroke of a pen. Kidnappers leave notes. Forgers sign phony checks.

FORENSIC 411

That's where a forensic document examiner's job begins. These experts can tell real documents from fake ones. With a good document expert on the case, criminals need to watch how they cross their *t*'s and dot their *i*'s.

IN THIS SECTION:

- how forensic document examiners REALLY TALK;
- what they look for in a PIECE OF EVIDENCE;
- who else is at the CRIME SCENE.

The Write Stuff

Forensic document examiners have their own way of talking. Find out what their vocabulary means.

signature
(SIG-nuh-chur) the special way that you sign your name, usually in cursive

forgery
(FORJ-ree) an illegal copy of someone's writing. Also fake money or paintings.

"This looks like Abraham Lincoln's signature to me. How can you tell it's a forgery?"

"We need to get someone in here to do a handwriting analysis on this document."

handwriting analysis
(HAND-rye-ting uh-NAL-uh-siss) the careful, step-by-step study of writing done by hand. It can be done to discover forgeries, or fakes.

document
(DOK-yoo-mehnt) a paper or collection of papers with any kind of writing on it

forensic document examiner
(fuh-REN-sik DOK-yoo-mehnt eg-ZAM-uhn-uhr) a person who uses scientific methods to study paperwork. A forensic document examiner is an expert in handwriting, paper, ink, stamps, typewriters, and computer printing.

"Find me a forensic document examiner. We need to know if this is real or not."

"I may be a forensic document examiner, but I don't believe in graphology."

graphology
(GRAF-ol-uh-gee) the study of handwriting to understand personality. Unlike forensic document examination, graphology is not a science.

Say What?

Here's some other lingo a forensic document examiner might use.

baseline
(BAYSS-line) the bottom of a line of writing
*"Look how her **baseline** goes up and down."*

known document
(nohn DOK-yoo-mehnt) a document everyone knows is real
*"This letter is a **known document** from Abraham Lincoln."*

pressure
(PRESH-ur) how hard the writer presses on the pen or pencil
*"Notice the heavy **pressure** on the capital letters. This guy nearly ripped the paper."*

questioned document
(KWES-chund DOK-yoo-mehnt) a document that may or may not be a forgery.
*"We think the **questioned document** is a fake."*

slant
(slant) to be at an angle
*"These letters **slant** to the right."*

What a Fake!

How do experts tell the real thing from a forgery?

Joseph Cosey is one of history's greatest fakers. He forged documents by Benjamin Franklin, Abraham Lincoln, and other famous people. Cosey died about 50 years ago. But his forgeries are still floating around today.

How would an expert tell a Cosey fake from the real thing?

It's a two-step process. First, document examiners look at the materials used to create the questioned document. They check to make sure the paper, ink, or stamps are from the right time period. Cosey was usually careful to use the right paper and ink.

Next they look at the writing itself. For this part of the examination they use a known document. That's a document everyone knows is real.

Examiners compare the two documents to see if the writing matches. Check out the list of some of the things they look for. **Then see how to tell a Cosey forgery from a Lincoln original.**

COSEY FORGERY

Cosey's letter was written slowly. Words are more up-and-down. They don't flow together.

1. How **SMOOTH** is the writing? Shaky writing can mean that someone is writing slowly—and faking someone else's handwriting.
2. What about the **SPACING** between letters and between the words? Are they the same in both documents?
3. What is the **HEIGHT** of the letters? Often forgers make their letters smaller than those of the person they're copying.
4. Does the writer **LIFT** his or her pen?
5. Does the writer **CONNECT** capital and lowercase letters?
6. How does the writer **FORM** the letters? Are any letters written in a strange way?
7. Does the writer put a lot of **PRESSURE** on his pen? Or does the writing seem light?
8. Which way do the letters **SLANT**?
9. Is the **BASELINE** straight or crooked? In other words, does the writer write in a straight line?
10. Does the writer have a **PARTICULAR** way of crossing *t*'s and dotting *i*'s?
11. Are the letters **CORRECTED** or traced over? This may be a sign of a forgery.

The letters are carefully written.

Please have this message
dispatched to Gen. Meade, and
give duplicate to the bearer,
Mrs. Morehead, a widow of
Culpepper County
Sep. 2, 1862 A. Lincoln

There isn't a lot of space between the lines.

All the letters of the signature are on the same line.

The Forensic Team

Forensic document examiners may work as part of a team to help solve crimes.

POLICE OFFICERS

They are often the ones to find, collect, and transport the evidence. They will call on a forensic document examiner if important papers are part of a crime.

FINGERPRINT SPECIALISTS

They find, photograph, and collect fingerprints found on forged documents. Then they compare them to people suspected of creating the forgery.

DETECTIVES OR AGENTS

They direct the crime investigation. They collect information about the crime, interview witnesses, identify suspects—and arrest them if there's enough evidence!

POSTAL INSPECTORS

They investigate mail-related crimes. They can help stop forgers who are selling fake documents through the mail.

LAWYERS

They argue criminal cases in court. District attorneys work for the state. They prosecute suspects. Defense lawyers defend suspects.

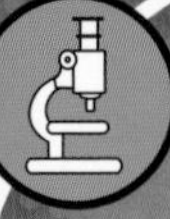

FORENSIC DOCUMENT EXAMINERS

They analyze written evidence to help solve crimes. Sometimes they decide whether a document is real or forged. Sometimes they try to match a suspect's handwriting with a piece of evidence.

TRUE-LIFE CASE FILES!

24 hours a day, 7 days a week, 365 days a year, forensic document examiners are solving mysteries.

IN THIS SECTION:

- a famous KIDNAPPING CASE is solved ... or is it?
- a FORGED SIGNATURE on a will tears a family apart;
- HISTORY is almost rewritten, thanks to a very skilled forger.

24/7 Science Behind the Scenes

Here's how forensic document examiners get the job done.

What does it take to solve a crime? Forensic document examiners don't just make guesses. They're like scientists. They follow a step-by-step process.

As you read the case studies, you can follow along with them. Keep an eye out for the icons below. They'll clue you in to each step along the way.

At the beginning of a case, document examiners identify ***one or two main questions*** they have to answer.

The next step is to ***gather and analyze evidence***. Document examiners collect as much information as they can. Then they study it to figure out what it means.

When they've studied all the data, document examiners ***come to a conclusion***. Is this document real—or a fake? If they can answer that question, they may have solved the case.

TRUE-LIFE CASE #1

Hopewell, New Jersey
March 1, 1932

The Lindbergh Kidnapping

It was a crime that shocked the world. Could handwriting analysis crack the case?

The Crime of the Century

The baby son of an American hero is stolen from his crib.

In 1932, everyone in America knew Charles Lindbergh's name. Five years earlier, he had flown across the Atlantic alone. Newspapers reported his feat around the world. Within days, he was a hero. Wherever he went, fans surrounded him.

Charles Lindbergh stands in front of his plane, the *Spirit of St. Louis.*

Lindbergh quickly got tired of the attention. He had a wife, Anne, and a baby named Charles Jr. He just wanted to be alone with his family. So he built a home in Hopewell, New Jersey. The house was hidden in the woods at the end of a long driveway.

But on March 1, 1932, the family's peace and quiet was shattered.

At 10 P.M., the family's nurse went to check on the Lindberghs' 20-month-old son. The boy wasn't in his crib! She ran to Charles's study. "Do you have the baby?" she asked, alarmed. "Please don't fool me."

The Lindberghs' home in Hopewell, New Jersey. Page 15 shows an aerial view of the house. See the second-floor window on the far left, near the chimney? That's the window from which the child was kidnapped.

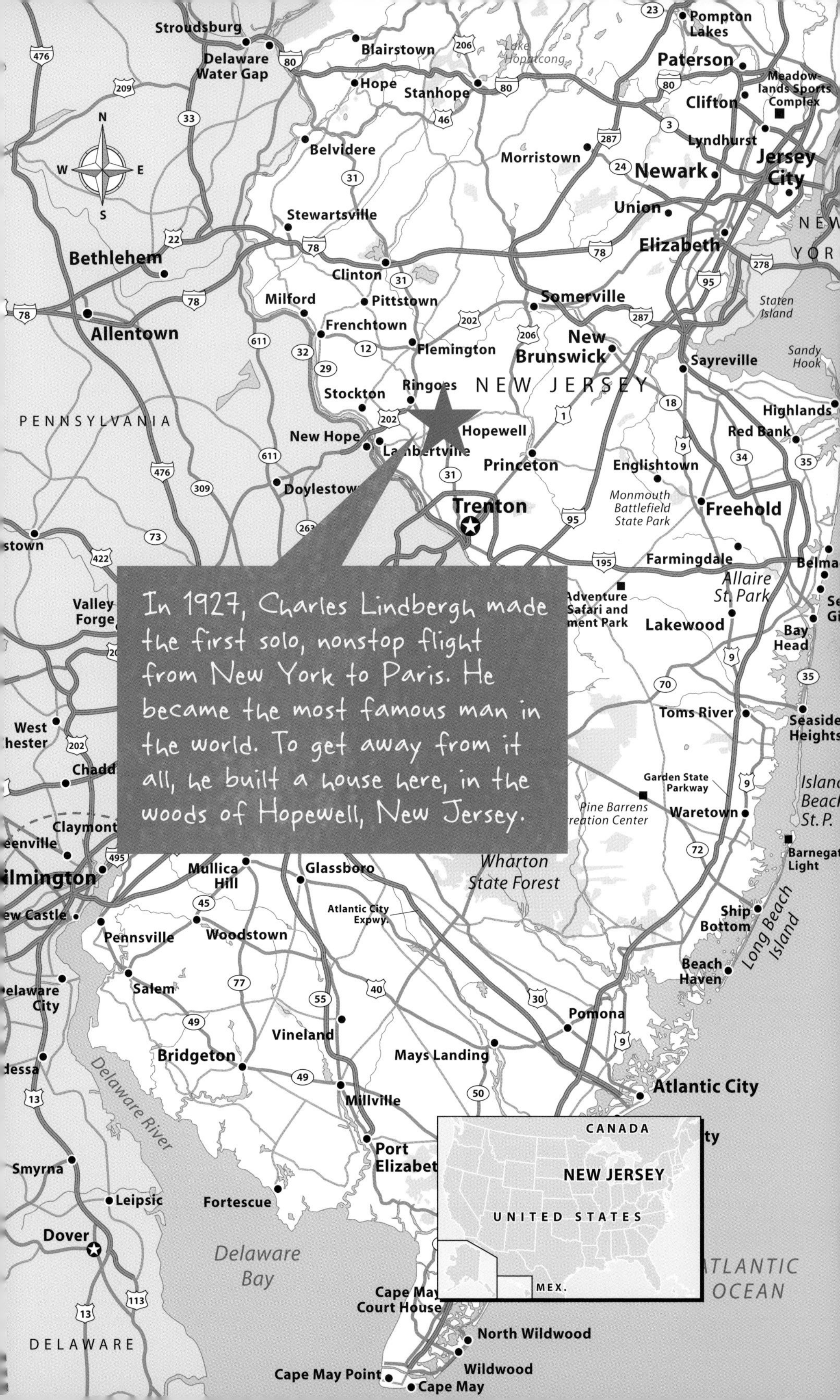
In 1927, Charles Lindbergh made the first solo, nonstop flight from New York to Paris. He became the most famous man in the world. To get away from it all, he built a house here, in the woods of Hopewell, New Jersey.
Stroudsburg
Delaware Water Gap
Blairstown
Pompton Lakes
Lake Hopatcong
Paterson
Hope
Stanhope
Meadowlands Sports Complex
Clifton
Belvidere
Morristown
Lyndhurst
Jersey City
Newark
N
W
E
S
Union
Stewartsville
Bethlehem
Elizabeth
Clinton
Milford
Pittstown
Somerville
Staten Island
Allentown
Frenchtown
New Brunswick
Flemington
Sayreville
Sandy Hook
Stockton
Ringoes
NEW JERSEY
PENNSYLVANIA
Highlands
Hopewell
Red Bank
New Hope
Princeton
Englishtown
Monmouth Battlefield State Park
Trenton
Freehold
Farmingdale
Allaire St. Park
Valley Forge
Adventure Safari and
Lakewood
Bay Head
Toms River
West
Garden State Parkway
Pine Barrens
Waretown
Claymont
Barnegat Light
Mullica Hill
Glassboro
Wharton State Forest
Atlantic City Expwy.
Ship Bottom
Long Beach Island
Pennsville
Woodstown
Beach Haven
Salem
Pomona
Vineland
Bridgeton
Mays Landing
Atlantic City
Millville
Delaware River
Port
Smyrna
Leipsic
Fortescue
Dover
Delaware Bay
CANADA
NEW JERSEY
UNITED STATES
MEX.
Cape May Court House
North Wildwood
Wildwood
Cape May Point
Cape May
DELAWARE
476
209
33
80
206
23
22
78
31
287
24
3
46
202
12
611
32
29
18
1
9
34
35
309
195
95
278
73
422
70
72
495
45
77
55
40
30
49
50
13
113

Lindbergh ran upstairs. He saw the empty crib. He saw an open window. "Anne!" he cried out to his wife. "They've stolen our baby."

At 10:25 P.M., Lindbergh called the New Jersey State police.

The Ransom Notes

A series of notes leads to an exchange of cash. But will Lindbergh find his son?

Police chiefs in more than 1400 cities received this poster about the Lindbergh baby kidnapping.

Police found two important clues that night. Near the Lindbergh home lay a homemade ladder. It was just tall enough to reach the baby's second-floor room.

The other clue was a note. Lindbergh had found it lying near the baby's window. Many of the words in the letter were spelled wrong:

> *Dear Sir!*
>
> *Have 50,000$ redy with 25000 in 20$ bills 15000$ in 10$ bills and 10000$ in 5$ bills. After 2-4 days we will inform you were to deliver the Mony.*
>
> *We warn you for making anyding public or for notify the polise the child is in gute care.*

On March 4 and 5, two more notes arrived. Both had words misspelled in similar ways. The second note, for instance, contained the words "everyding," "mony," and "gut." The kidnapper raised the **ransom** to $70,000.

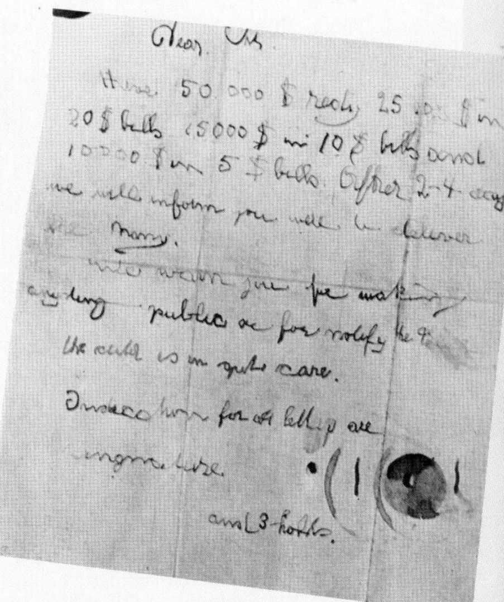
Dear Sir!
Have 50.000$ redy 25 000$ in
20$ bills 15000$ in 10$ bills and
10000$ in 5$ bills. After 2-4 days
we will inform you were to deliver
the mony.
We warn you for making
anyding public or for notify the Police
the child is in gute care.
Indication for all letters are
singnature
and 3 holes.

The first ransom note sent to the Lindberghs. This handwritten note would later be used as evidence against the main suspect in the kidnapping.

Lindbergh decided he wanted to pay. He sent messages to the **kidnapper** in newspaper ads. The kidnapper wrote back to arrange a meeting. Lindbergh gathered $70,000 in cash. He used special bills called gold certificates. The certificates would be easier to trace than regular bills.

On April 2, Lindbergh and a friend drove to a graveyard. In the darkness, they met a man who called himself "John." Lindbergh's friend handed over the money. John handed back a note. The baby was fine, the note said. He was on a boat called *Nelly*.

Lindbergh was overjoyed. Soon he would have his son back. Lindbergh spent several weeks flying up and down the East Coast. But he couldn't find the *Nelly*.

On May 12, 1932, the search ended. A truck driver was walking in the woods just two miles (3 km) from the Lindbergh home. He found the body of a baby. It was little Charles.

Reading Between the Lines

Who are police looking for? Handwriting experts lead the way.

With the sad news, the **investigation** changed. Now police were looking for a murderer. And the whole world was watching.

Police sent the ransom notes to two **experts**, Dr. Wilmer T. Souder and Albert S. Osborn.

They wanted several questions answered. Were the notes written by a single kidnapper? Or were police looking for a gang of criminals? Could the experts tell anything about the writer from the notes?

Souder and Osborn sat down with the notes. Here are some of the things they noticed:

The ransom notes became important in the trial of the suspected kidnapper. As shown here, words from the ransom note were compared to words written by the suspect.

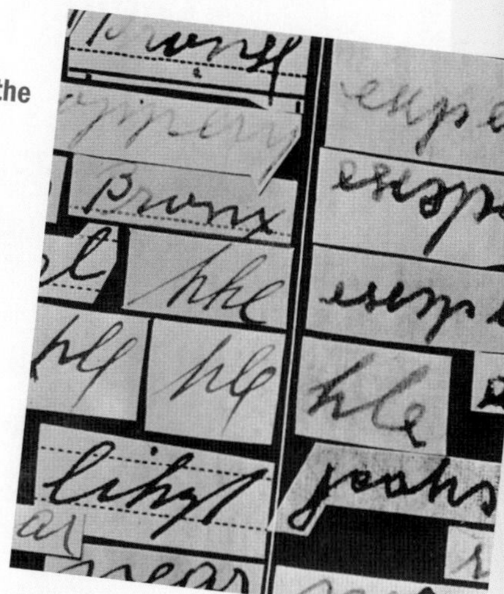

- Words were misspelled in the same ways in all the notes. *Mony*, *singnature*, and *ingnore* were a few examples.
- Words like *light* and *right* were written with the *g* and *h* reversed.
- The *t*'s were not crossed. The *i*'s and *j*'s were not dotted.

Both Souder and Osborn reached the same conclusion. One person had written all of the ransom notes.

Osborn went one step further. He thought the writer was German. The notes included the words *gut*, *aus*, and *dank*. These are the German words for *good*, *our*, and *thank*.

Osborn made up a paragraph with some of the key words in it. He told police to read it aloud to any **suspects** they found. The suspects would have to write down the words. Police would then look for two things. Did the handwriting match the writing in the ransom notes? Did it contain the same mistakes?

Suspect Arrested!

The police follow a trail of cash. Will it lead to the real kidnapper?

For two years, the investigation stalled. But the ransom money was still out there. All $70,000 of it.

Finally, police got a hot lead. In September 1934, a gas station manager took a $10 gold certificate from a customer. He stared at it. The government had stopped using these bills a year before. Was it fake?

"What's wrong?" asked the driver in a German accent. The manager said nothing was wrong. But as the car pulled away, he wrote the license plate number down on the bill. Then he deposited the money in the bank.

The bank clerk was also curious. He checked a booklet that the **FBI** had printed. The booklet contained all the **serial numbers** of the Lindbergh ransom bills. The bill was a match!

Police traced the license number to the owner of the car. His name was Bruno Richard Hauptmann. Hauptmann was a German-born carpenter. Police arrested him. Was he the "John" who took the ransom bills that night in the graveyard? Both Lindbergh and his friend said he was.

Police searched Hauptmann's home. They found $14,000 of the ransom cash hidden in the garage. They also found a missing **beam** in the attic. The wood from the remaining beams matched the wood on the homemade ladder.

Hauptmann insisted he was innocent. He said that a friend named Isidor Fisch had given him the money for safekeeping. Fisch had gone back to Germany a few months before. Hauptmann said he knew nothing about the kidnapping.

What would his handwriting say to police?

Bruno Hauptmann, shortly after his arrest. He swore that he had nothing to do with the Lindbergh baby kidnapping.

The police dug up Bruno Hauptmann's garage. There, they found part of the ransom money.

Handwriting on Trial

Does Hauptmann's writing match the ransom notes?

Police questioned Hauptmann for a long time. Then they made him write for hours. He copied Osborn's sample paragraph. He also copied some of the ransom notes. Police made him do each test three times, with three different pens.

Investigators also gathered writing **evidence** from Hauptmann's home. The experts compared the evidence with the ransom notes.

- Hauptmann wrote the words *to* and *the* in unusual ways. So did the note-writer.
- Hauptmann's *y* looked like a *j*. The note-writer's did, too.

Osborn, Souder and several other experts all reached the same conclusion: Hauptmann had written the ransom notes.

Osborn and Souder testified against Hauptmann at the trial.

The defense produced one handwriting expert. His name was John Trendley. Trendley said he doubted that Hauptmann wrote the first ransom note. Would the **jury** agree?

Forensic handwriting expert Albert S. Osborn. He was one of the experts who analyzed the ransom notes. He also analyzed Hauptmann's handwriting. He testified in court that Hauptmann had most likely written the ransom notes.

Guilty!

Hauptmann is convicted. So why is the case still a mystery?

The jury took just 11 hours to come to a decision. They found Hauptmann guilty. On April 3, 1936, he was executed for the murder of Charles Lindbergh Jr.

Still, many people think the full story hasn't been told. Hauptmann's friend Isidor Fisch died in Germany in 1934. No one ever had a chance to question him. And where was the rest of the cash? Police were under a lot of pressure to find the kidnapper. Did they frame Hauptmann?

Today, handwriting experts still puzzle over the case. The Court TV show *Forensic Files* sent the handwriting evidence to three experts. They all came to the same conclusion: The same person wrote the ransom notes. And that person was probably Bruno Richard Hauptmann. 24/7

Hauptmann's friend Isidor Fisch. Hauptmann said that Fisch had asked him to keep the money for him. Fisch then left for Germany. The police never questioned him.

Mark Walch talks about new computer software developed to analyze the Lindbergh ransom notes.

24/7: **Are you a document examiner?**
WALCH: No. I'm a director of Gannon Technologies. We created the new software program.

24/7: **What can this new software do?**
WALCH: We are training the computer to tell us who wrote [a document].

24/7: **How does it work?**
WALCH: There are certain measurements in handwriting that stay the same for any one person. This program can take 20 measurements of your small *a*, for example. Then, when it looks at another *a*, it can figure out how likely it is that you wrote that one.

24/7: **Why is it important for a computer to do this work?**
WALCH: This program makes document examination more scientific. That will help make document examiners' testimony more believable.

24/7: **Could this software replace people?**
WALCH: No. It's just another tool for forensic document examiners to use.

In the Lindbergh case, experts linked a kidnapper to ransom notes. In the next case, a team finds out if a woman's will has been faked.

TRUE-LIFE CASE #2

Canterbury, Kent, England
April 2002–November 2004

The Grandmother, the Will, and the Brand-New Porsche

Phyllis Davis died and left a fortune to her grandchildren. But who actually signed her will?

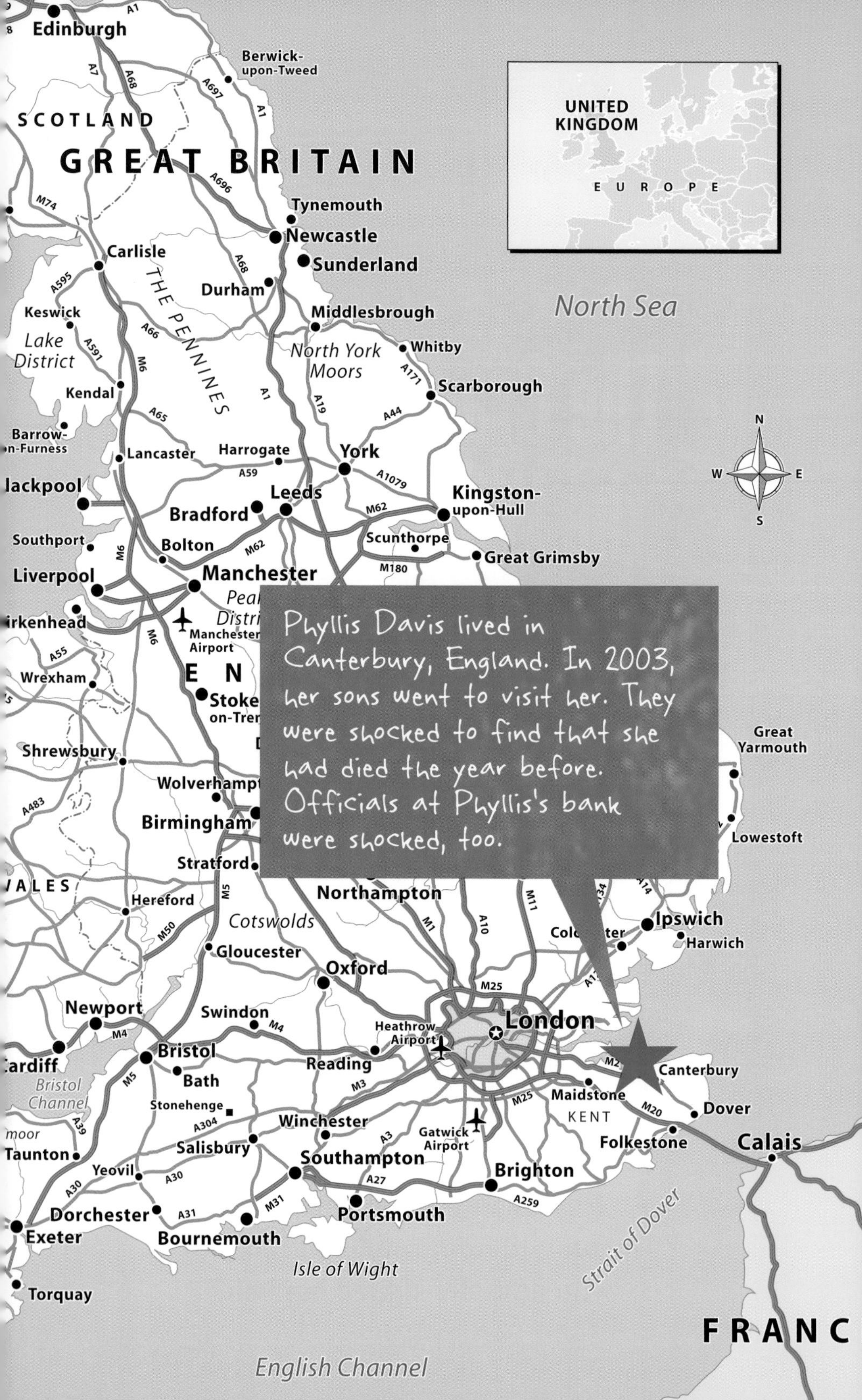

Phyllis Davis lived in Canterbury, England. In 2003, her sons went to visit her. They were shocked to find that she had died the year before. Officials at Phyllis's bank were shocked, too.

Family Feud

Divorce leads to division. What will happen to the fortune?

Members of the Davis family were not close. Brothers Christopher and Robin Davis once stopped speaking to each other for 15 years. Neither of them got along well with their mother, Phyllis Davis.

In 1998, things got worse for Robin. He divorced his wife, Linda. Linda and the couple's two children stayed close to Phyllis. Robin did not.

Still, in 2003, Robin and Christopher went to visit their mother. They arrived at her home in Canterbury, England. But Phyllis was gone—for good. A neighbor told them the news. Their mother had died the previous spring at the age of 87.

Robin and Christopher were shocked. Their own mother had been dead for a year! Why hadn't anyone told them? And what happened to her money?

Phyllis Davis's house in Canterbury, England. She died in 2002. However, her sons did not find out about her death until 2003.

Last Wishes

The Davis brothers discover two wills. Were they both written by their mother?

Robin and Christopher knew that their mother, Phyllis, had written a **will** in 1989. She had told them about it. She had about 420,000 **pounds** ($790,000) in cash and property. The will left most of that to them.

Phyllis Davis's first will left most of her money to her sons. The second will left most of it to her grandchildren and her daughter-in-law.

But now there was a new will. It was dated March 2002. That was just a month before Phyllis died. The will had been written on a home computer. It had Phyllis's signature on it. The new will left 25,000 pounds ($47,000) each to Robin, Christopher, and a **charity** for the blind.

All the rest of Phyllis Davis's money went to Linda and her two kids, Richard and Vicky.

That wasn't the only shock. The brothers went to Phyllis's bank. Strangely, their mother's bank account was still open. And Robin's 26-year-old son, Richard, was handling the money.

The brothers learned that Richard had mailed in documents with his grandmother's signature on them. These documents gave him control of her bank account. They were dated a month before Phyllis's death. But the bank didn't get them until after she died.

Robin and Christopher asked to see the records for their mother's account. At the end of 2002, someone had spent 15,000 pounds ($28,000) to buy a new Porsche. It was bought after Phyllis Davis died.

Someone had bought a new Porsche with Phyllis's money. And it was bought after Phyllis died!

Dead people don't drive Porsches.

The brothers called the police.

THE FAMILY FEUD

Phyllis wasn't talking to her sons, Robin and Christopher. But she was still close to her former daughter-in-law, Linda, and to her grandkids, Richard and Vicky.

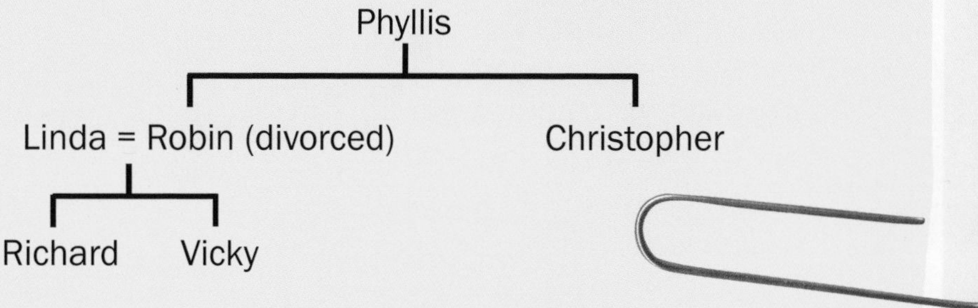

The Investigation Begins

The police begin to question the suspects—and the documents.

Police paid a visit to Phyllis's grandson, Richard Davis. Richard explained that Phyllis had changed her will just before she died.

Investigators questioned Richard about the will itself. It had been written on a laptop computer and signed in ink.

Richard admitted that he had written the will on his computer. He said his grandmother had asked him to do it.

Police took a look at Richard's computer. It came from an office where Richard used to work. He admitted stealing the computer from his former boss.

The evidence was piling up. But police still had to deal with the bank paperwork and the second will. Both documents had Phyllis Davis's signature on them.

Or did they?

Richard Davis admitted to writing his grandmother's will on his computer. And he admitted that he had stolen that computer!

Stop Sign

Experts take a close look at the signatures. Are they real, or are they forgeries?

The police called on handwriting expert Barry Taylor. It was Taylor's job to figure out if the signatures were real.

Taylor had two questioned documents. He had the will and the bank paperwork that gave Richard control of Phyllis's money.

Now he needed known documents. The investigators collected examples of Phyllis Davis's signature. They made sure to find

AGING SIGNATURES

John Adams was the second President of the U.S. He held office from 1797 to 1801. Like most people's signatures, his changed as he got older.

John Adams

This signature was written in 1803. The writing is still clear and smooth.

John Adams

This one was written in 1819, when Adams was 84. By then his signature had become shaky.

samples written just before Phyllis died. Handwriting can become shaky as someone grows old.

Investigators also collected samples of writing by Richard Davis and Linda Davis.

Finally Taylor sat down to compare the samples. He decided that Phyllis Davis had not signed the documents herself. The signatures had been forged. Richard Davis was ruled out as the suspected forger. Linda Davis was not.

Based on this evidence, mother and son were arrested. They were later found guilty of faking the second will. Christopher and Robin Davis got most of their mother's money. 24/7

Richard Davis and Linda Davis. At their trial, a handwriting expert said that it was "distinctly possible" that Linda had signed the will. The judge called Richard Davis "a thoroughly dishonest young man."

Case #2 involved two fake signatures. The next case involves 40 volumes of a diary! How did the experts handle it?

TRUE-LIFE CASE #3

Berlin, Germany;
Boernersdorf, Germany
1981–1983

The Case of the Hitler Diaries

The German dictator terrorized the world during World War II. More than 35 years later, a collector produced 40 notebooks. Were they really Hitler's diaries?

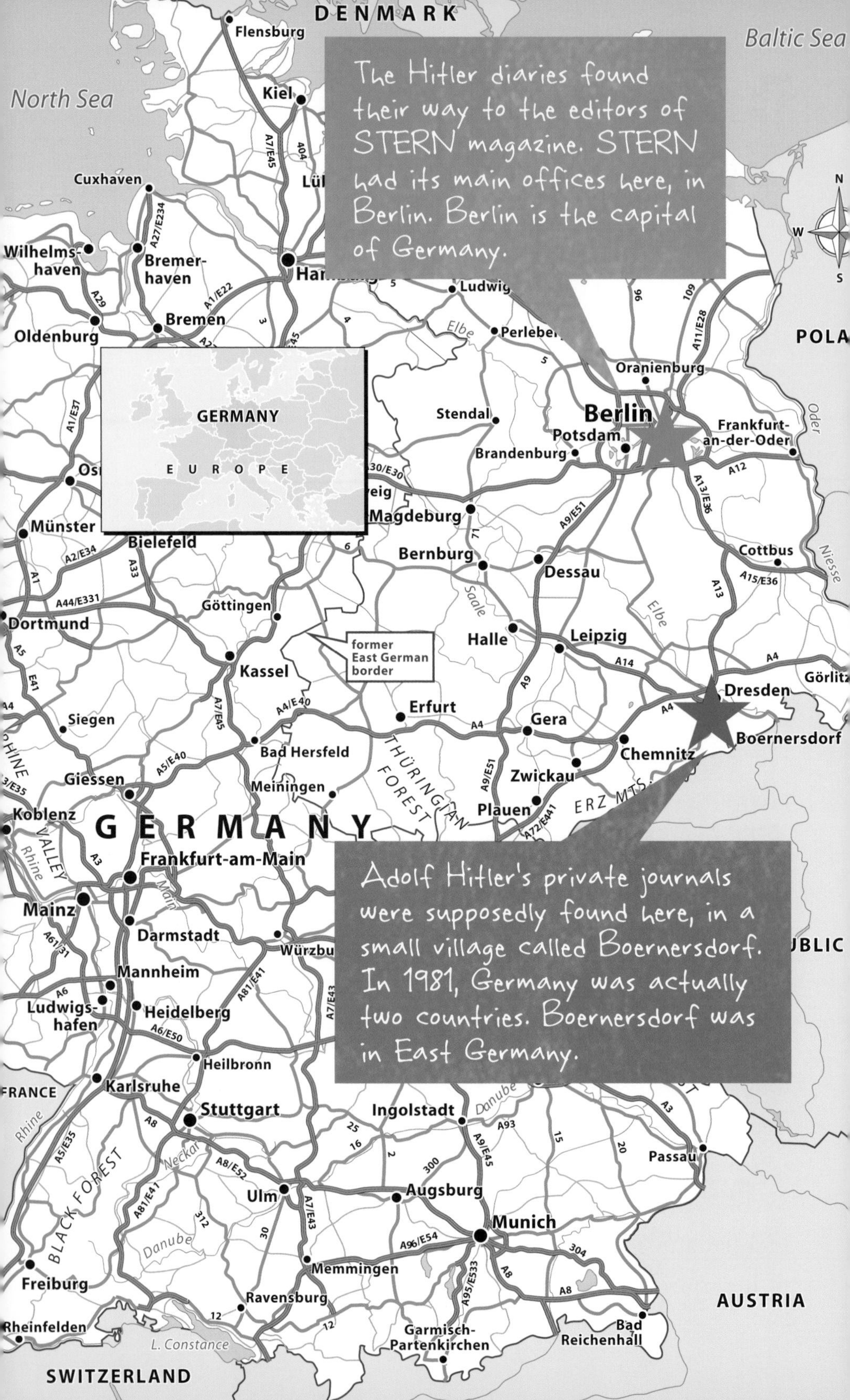

The Hitler diaries found their way to the editors of STERN magazine. STERN had its main offices here, in Berlin. Berlin is the capital of Germany.
Adolf Hitler's private journals were supposedly found here, in a small village called Boernersdorf. In 1981, Germany was actually two countries. Boernersdorf was in East Germany.
DENMARK
Baltic Sea
North Sea
POLA
FRANCE
SWITZERLAND
AUSTRIA
UBLIC
GERMANY
EUROPE
GERMANY
former East German border
Flensburg
Kiel
Cuxhaven
Wilhelms-haven
Bremer-haven
Bremen
Oldenburg
Ludwig
Perleber
Oranienburg
Stendal
Berlin
Potsdam
Brandenburg
Frankfurt-an-der-Oder
Magdeburg
Münster
Bielefeld
Bernburg
Dessau
Cottbus
Göttingen
Dortmund
Halle
Leipzig
Kassel
Dresden
Görlitz
Erfurt
Gera
Siegen
Bad Hersfeld
Chemnitz
Boernersdorf
Giessen
Meiningen
Zwickau
Koblenz
Plauen
ERZ MTS.
THÜRINGIAN FOREST
Frankfurt-am-Main
Mainz
Darmstadt
Würzbu
Mannheim
Ludwigs-hafen
Heidelberg
Heilbronn
Karlsruhe
Stuttgart
Ingolstadt
Passau
Ulm
Augsburg
Munich
BLACK FOREST
Memmingen
Freiburg
Ravensburg
Garmisch-Partenkirchen
Bad Reichenhall
Rheinfelden
L. Constance
Elbe
Saale
Oder
Niesse
Rhine
Main
Danube
Neckar

The Diaries of Adolf Hitler?

The diaries appeared 35 years after his death.

In 1981, the editors of *Stern*, a German magazine, found the story of a lifetime.

A journalist named Gerd Heidemann said he had a secret source. The source had found some handwritten notebooks. The notebooks were diaries of one of history's worst dictators: German leader Adolf Hitler.

Heidemann said *Stern* could buy the diaries. The deal would be expensive—$2 million. But to the editors, it was worth it.

During the 1930s and '40s, Hitler terrorized Europe. In 1939, he started World War II. He launched a secret plan to rid Europe of Jews and other minorities.

The Allies finally defeated Germany in 1945. By that time, Hitler had killed 11 million people. Six million of his victims were Jews.

Why did Hitler commit such terrible crimes? What went on inside his mind? Maybe the diaries would give some answers.

The editors of *Stern* decided to buy the diaries. They gave Heidemann some money to give to his source.

German dictator Adolf Hitler was known for his long, emotional speeches. Had he also been keeping a diary?

Secret Scoop

The editors call in handwriting experts. But are they given the right tools?

Before they published the diaries, the editors needed to make sure they were real.

Heidemann's story seemed to make sense. He named his source as Konrad Fischer. Fischer collected and sold World War II **artifacts**. The diaries supposedly came from a little town called Boernersdorf. A plane crashed there at the end of World War II. For years, people had claimed that the plane contained some of Hitler's belongings.

Journalist Gerd Heidemann *(above)* was the middle man between *Stern* magazine and a man named Konrad Fischer. Fischer claimed he had diaries written by Adolf Hitler.

According to Fischer, a fireproof metal chest survived the crash. Farmers hid the chest. Eventually, they sneaked it out of the country. Now, Fischer had found the owner.

It was a good story. But *Stern*'s editors needed proof. To get it, they called two handwriting experts. They contacted Dr. Max Frei-Sulzer from Switzerland, and Ordway Hilton from South Carolina.

The editors gave each of the experts two pages from the notebooks. The experts were asked to compare these pages with seven samples of Hitler's writing. Fischer provided some of the samples from his own collection. The rest came from a library.

The experts had to answer one important question. Were the questioned documents—Fischer's pages—written by the same person who wrote the known documents?

The Investigation

The verdict is in: According to experts, Hitler wrote the diaries.

THE EVIDENCE

The editors flew to Switzerland and to South Carolina. They hand-delivered the documents to both experts.

Right away, Hilton noticed something. Not all the signatures in the known documents matched. But Hilton didn't worry. People's signatures tend to change over time.

Hilton spent three and a half weeks working on his report. He used a **binocular microscope** to analyze

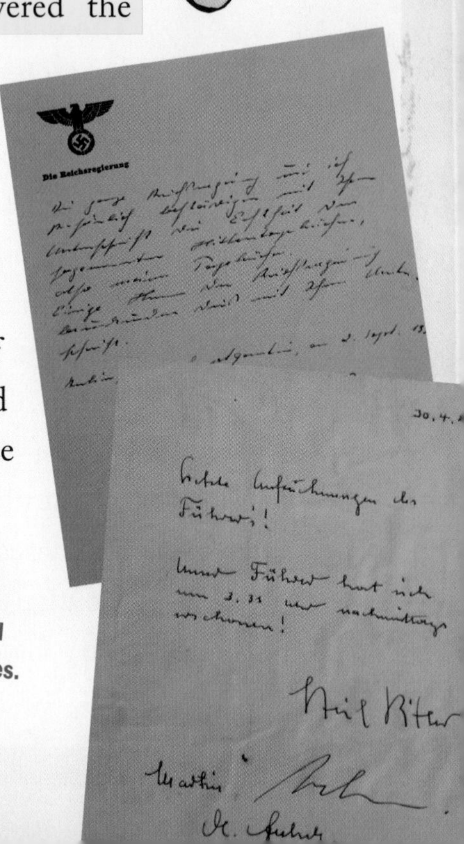

Above: **A so-called known document written by Adolf Hitler.** ***Below:*** **A questioned page from one of the diaries. Both were provided to the handwriting experts by Konrad Fischer.**

the writing. The pages showed "a free, natural form of writing," Hilton said.

Frei-Sulzer spent an even longer time on the two pages. He noted how unusual Hitler's *I*'s, *H*'s and *T*'s were. He took pictures of the letters and enlarged them. He examined them.

Both experts came to the same conclusion. The two questioned documents were real.

Konrad Fischer was the man who claimed to have found the Hitler diaries. Here, he holds up a copy of the issue of *Stern* magazine with the diaries. Fischer's real name was actually Konrad Kujau.

Too Good to Be True?

The diaries are published. And the reaction isn't what *Stern* had hoped.

On April 25, 1983, *Stern* printed the diaries. The event made headlines all over the world. But soon the diaries and the magazine were under attack. Historians said the diaries had to be fakes. The diaries didn't match what was known about Hitler.

First of all, people who were close to Hitler said he didn't keep a diary. Second, people said Hitler seemed too nice in the diaries!

Other mistakes were more obvious. The diary had several dates of Hitler's speeches

Handwriting expert Kenneth Rendell was the last expert brought in to examine the diaries. He knew immediately that something was wrong.

wrong. Why would Hitler make such mistakes?

Stern's editors defended the diaries. By now, Heidemann had brought them more than 40 notebooks. They had paid him over $2 million.

But then they decide to let one more expert take a look.

The expert's name was Kenneth Rendell. And as soon as he saw the diaries, he thought they were fakes. "Even at first glance everything looked wrong," he wrote later. The paper was cheap. The ink looked modern. The signatures looked fake to him.

Rendell had brought a thick folder with copies of pages known to be by Hitler. He had one of the notebooks photocopied. Then, he and his assistant cut out all of the capital letters. They pasted them onto sheets of paper. They did the same thing for other letters and symbols.

They compared these letters to letters from known Hitler documents. The capital letters *E*, *H*, and *K* in the diary looked nothing like Hitler's writing. Even someone who wasn't an expert could see the truth: The diaries were clearly fakes.

Case Closed

The forger is arrested. How did he fool the world?

How did the other experts make such a big mistake? The known documents they analyzed were flawed. Some of them came from Konrad Fischer. They were fakes, just like the diaries. Of course they looked like the diaries. They had been forged by the same person—Konrad Fischer!

The police got busy. They started a search for Fischer and Gerd Heidemann. Eventually, the two men were brought to trial. Both were sentenced to four years in prison. 24/7

Time magazine reported the hoax in the May 16, 1983, issue. One of the biggest stories of the century had turned out to be one of the biggest scams of the century.

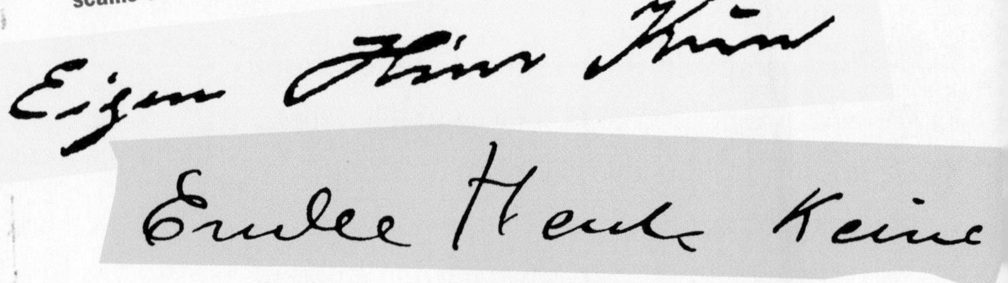

The forger's handwriting is on top. Hitler's handwriting is below. See how the _E_'s, _H_'s, and _K_'s are different?

FORENSIC DOWNLOAD

Are you writing all this down? Here's more about the past, present, and future of handwriting analysis.

IN THIS SECTION:

- a FORGER helps one country take over another—and other notes from the past;
- forensic document examination MAKES HEADLINES;
- a look at the TOOLS that examiners use;
- is forensic document examination in YOUR FUTURE?

1450s And Scotland Belongs to ...

For hundreds of years, English kings ruled Scotland. The Scots resisted. But in the mid-1400s, England gets some help from a forger. John Hardyng fakes old documents and maps. The forgeries support England's right to rule Scotland. The **scam** isn't discovered until the 1600s.

1 Key Dates in

2

1850s–1870s Founding Father Forger

A forger named Robert Spring makes a career imitating George Washington's handwriting. Spring personalizes his fakes. He targets wealthy people. Then he offers them forged letters from Washington—addressed to their **ancestors**. One of his forgeries was displayed in Philadelphia's Independence Hall!

3

1910 Documents Dude

Albert S. Osborn publishes the book *Questioned Documents*. It becomes the bible for forensic document examiners. Osborn is shown above on the left. He is with his son, Albert Osborn, who was also a handwriting expert.

4

1930s Rewriting History

Joseph Cosey *(above)* rises to fame as a forger. He fakes documents by Abraham Lincoln, Mark Twain, and others. Cosey uses a large collection of pens, inks, and historical papers in his work. Today, his forgeries are collector's items. Could someone get rich forging Cosey forgeries?

1935 Trial of the Century
Bruno Hauptmann is found guilty in a famous kidnapping case. He is later executed for murdering the son of famous pilot Charles Lindbergh. At his trial, handwriting experts claimed that the ransom notes were written by Hauptmann.

See Case #1: The Lindbergh Kidnapping.

Forensic Document Examination

Handwriting analysis is old school—really, really old school! Find out about its history.

6

1970s What Nerve!
Clifford Irving publishes the fake autobiography of Howard Hughes. At the time, Hughes was one of the richest men in the world—and still fully alive. He never went out in public or talked to the press. Irving was hoping Hughes wouldn't comment on the book. But Hughes did—and Irving went to jail

7

1980s Hitler Diaries
Stern magazine in Germany publishes what editors believe are Adolf Hitler's diaries. The diaries are later found to be fake.

See Case #3: The Case of the Hitler Diaries.

8

1985 Mormon Forgeries
Forger Mark Hofmann is sentenced to life in prison. Hofmann *(right)* faked important documents in the history of the Mormon church. For years, he fooled everyone. Then church leaders began to catch on. Hofmann set off several bombs in Salt Lake City, Utah. He eventually killed two people and injured himself.

In the News

Read all about it! Forensic document examination is in the news.

Study Says Handwriting Analysis Works

For years, handwriting analysis was an art. It depended on the human eye—and a good magnifying glass. Now, computer programs are turning it into a science.

NEW YORK CITY—July 2002

Handwriting analysis has often been called an art, not a science. A new study suggests it might be more scientific than people think. The study was published in the *Journal of Forensic Sciences* this month.

Researchers had 1,500 people copy four paragraphs three times each. The results were scanned into a computer. The computer measured the size and shape of all the letters. It measured the distance between letters. It measured the pressure each writer put on the pen.

Using the measurements, researchers guessed which samples were written by the same person. They guessed correctly a surprising 98 percent of the time.

Actors Gary Dourdan *(above)*, William Petersen, and Marg Helgenberger *(right)* from *CSI: Crime Scene Investigation*. Because of this show, many juries now expect high-tech scientific evidence.

The CSI Effect

DEERFIELD, ILLINOIS—May 2006

Every week 60 million TV viewers tune in to *CSI: Crime Scene Investigation*. On the show, investigators use high-tech forensic science to solve crimes. Each week, they put a criminal behind bars. And each week, it's the science that breaks the case.

In the real world, it doesn't always work that way. But jury members have begun to expect scientific evidence in real-life criminal trials.

How should police departments and lawyers respond? A magazine called *Law and Order* says they shouldn't get pushed around by the "CSI Effect."

Sometimes low-tech skills are more important than, say, **DNA** testing. Often, forgery and **fraud** are a department's most common crimes. If so, the magazine says, they should train handwriting analysts, not DNA experts!

Reading Between the Lines

Have a look at the tools and equipment used by forensic document examiners.

magnifying glass A document examiner's most basic tool. It's used to look closely at individual letters.

binocular microscope
This tool gives a really close-up view. Experts use it to examine the ink used in a questioned document. It also helps reveal whether the letters have been traced.

ruler Another basic tool. It's used to measure margins and baselines.

protractor
Experts use a protractor to measure the slant of a writer's letters.

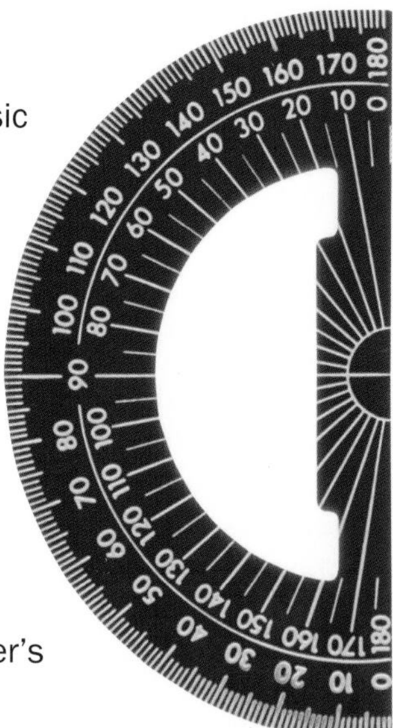

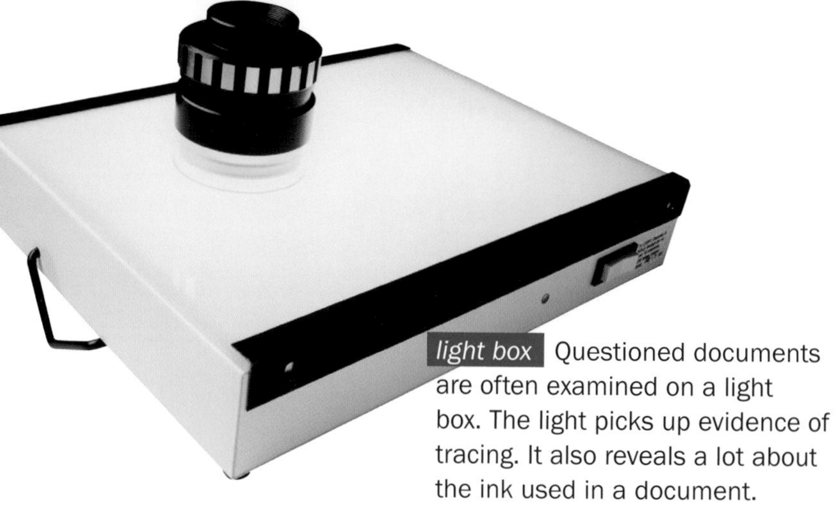

light box Questioned documents are often examined on a light box. The light picks up evidence of tracing. It also reveals a lot about the ink used in a document.

different light sources Different kinds of light can help identify various kinds of ink. They can also show changes made to a piece of paper. Infrared and ultraviolet are two kinds of light that forensic document examiners use.

cameras Experts may photograph questioned and known documents. They use the images to compare the two documents.

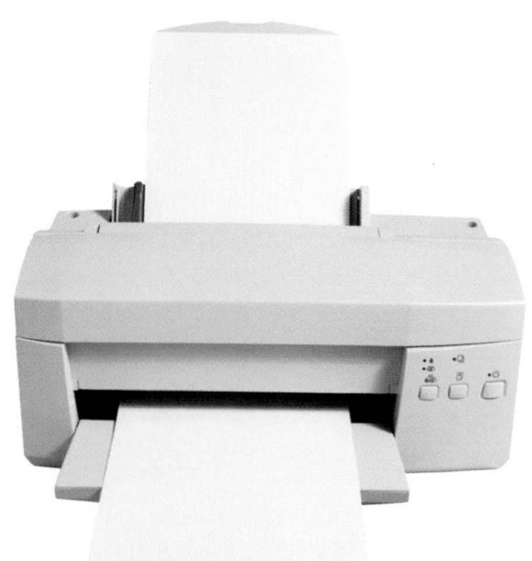

computer printers / copiers / faxes / staplers Good document examiners keep up with the latest technologies. Often they can trace a document to the machine that produced it.

What Does Your Handwriting Say About You?

Graphology is not a science. But it's pretty fun. Here's a guide to analyzing your own handwriting.

Graphologists say that your handwriting is your "brainwriting." They believe you express your personality in the way that you write. Do you believe it, too?

Test some of their theories for yourself. Look at a page of your own handwriting on unlined paper. Then answer the questions below.

1 Where do you cross your *t*'s?

- *3/4 of the way up:* You're realistic about your goals.
- *very high:* You're reaching for the stars.
- *very low:* You could be feeling down.

2 How do you dot your *i*'s?

- *close to the stem:* You're very detailed.
- *high over the stem:* You're patient with details.
- *missing completely:* You have trouble remembering things you're supposed to finish.
- *with a circle:* You want to stand out, but you're also looking for acceptance.

FOCUSED realistic

3 What does your Personal Pronoun I (PPI) look like?

- *well balanced, with both an upper loop and a lower hook:* You probably have a good relationship with your mom and dad.
- *a "stick figure," written with a single stroke:* You're an independent person.
- *printed, not in cursive:* Another sign of independence.

- *very large:* You're confident and take up a lot of personal space.

- *very small:* You don't like to draw a lot of attention to yourself.

4 How crowded is your writing?

- *very crowded:* You may be shy and withdrawn.

crowded

- *takes up the whole page:* You have a lot of confidence.

whole page

5 How big are your letters?

- *small and neat:* You are very focused and controlled.

small and neat

- *huge:* Chances are you're loose and carefree.

huge

6 Do you write the way you were taught in school?

- *yes, the letters look perfect:* You're good at following rules.

perfect

- *no, the letters are unusual:* You're very creative.

unusual

- *no, the writing is sloppy:* You may not be well organized.

7 What do the margins look like?

- *even and consistent:* You're a careful planner.
- *narrow:* You may take on more than you can handle.
- *wide:* You're cautious and put strict limits on yourself.

What do you think? Does your **analysis** fit you to a "t"? Or are you ready to write off graphology as just another phony science?

HELP WANTED: Forensic Document Examiner

Interested in forensic document examination? Here's more information about the field.

Q&A: GRANT SPERRY

Grant Sperry runs the federal document lab in Memphis, Tennessee. He's also a private forensic document examiner.

24/7: How did you get started?

SPERRY: I was a special agent with the Army Criminal Investigations Command. I developed an interest in all types of frauds.

24/7: What other training have you done?

SPERRY: I did a two-year training with the Army Lab. I've done courses with the **CIA**, the **Secret Service**, the FBI. You have to constantly keep educating yourself.

24/7: What do you like about your job?

SPERRY: I learn something new on every single case. And I get great satisfaction out of solving issues in a way that helps somebody. Every morning I wake up and think, "I get to go to the lab."

To see Grant Sperry's complete report on the Lindbergh case, go to www.forensicfiles.com/onehourspecials.htm

24/7: You analyzed the ransom notes from the Lindbergh case. What was that like?

SPERRY: I was surprised by how much evidence there was! I used software called Write On. That really helped my analysis. Once I scanned in all the documents, I could do searches. I could ask for all the *th* combinations, for instance. Then I could compare them all.

24/7: What did you learn about the kidnapper Bruno Hauptmann?

SPERRY: He **disguised** his handwriting the same way—every time. That's very unusual. He probably did something very simple, like holding the pen differently. That way it's easy to write the same way every time.

THE STATS

DAY JOB

- Very few forensic document examiners work alone. Most work for the police, the FBI, or the Secret Service. They may specialize in document analysis. But many also work as regular officers or agents.

MONEY

- Police officers average between $34,000 and $56,000 a year. FBI agents start at $48,000 a year.

EDUCATION

- 4 years of college
- 2 years of full-time training in a recognized document laboratory. Many forensic document examiners get their training on the job. The FBI and the U.S. Secret Service have their own schools.
- Certification by the American Board of Forensic Document Examiners (ABFDE)

THE NUMBERS

- Only 41 forensic document examiners have private practices in the U.S. The ABFDE certifies 126 examiners.

24/7: What do you have to say to young people who might be interested in forensic document examination?

SPERRY: Great! We need more good forensic scientists. Go to the the American Academy of Forensic Science Web site. It's www.aafs.org. We have a Young Forensic Scientists Forum. It will tell you how to get involved in the subject.

DO YOU HAVE WHAT IT TAKES?

Take this totally unscientific quiz to find out if forensic document examination might be a good career for you.

1. **How do you think you'd feel about speaking in a courtroom?**
   a) I'd love for everyone to listen to what I have to say!
   b) Well, I guess I could get used to it!
   c) I'd try to avoid it as much as possible.

2. **Are you good at noticing details?**
   a) Yes, I look closely at things to see every detail.
   b) Sometimes, but I miss things occasionally.
   c) No, I'm bored by details.

3. **Do you like to study history?**
   a) Yes, I love understanding what happened in the past.
   b) Sometimes, but I don't remember the dates.
   c) Not really. I just don't find it that interesting.

4. **Are you interested in literature and reading?**
   a) I love reading. When I find an author I like, I read everything she's written.
   b) Sometimes I like to read. But not all the time.
   c) I'm not really interested in books.

5. **Are you interested in solving crimes?**
   a) Yes. I want criminals put in jail.
   b) I like to watch crime shows on TV.
   c) Someone else can do that.

6. **Do you like technology?**
   a) It's really cool. I love learning the latest about computers and video.
   b) It's OK. I can work with it when I need to.
   c) It's not interesting at all to me. I try to avoid it.

YOUR SCORE

Give yourself 3 points for every "**a**" you chose. Give yourself 2 points for every "**b**" you chose. Give yourself 1 point for every "**c**" you chose.

If you got **15–18 points**, you'd probably be a good forensic document examiner. If you got **11–14 points**, you might be a good forensic document examiner. If you got **6–10 points**, you might want to look at another career!

HOW TO GET STARTED...NOW!

It's never too early to start working toward your goals.

GET AN EDUCATION

- Take science and history classes. Document analysts use chemistry to examine inks and paper. A knowledge of history helps tell the old from the new.
- Start thinking about college. Look for schools with a good forensic science or criminal justice program. None of them have majors in document examination. But many have courses on the subject.
- Read the newspaper. Keep up with what's going on in your community.
- Read anything you can find about forensic document examination and history. See the books and Web sites in the Resources section on pages 56–58.
- Graduate from high school!

NETWORK!

- Find out about forensic groups in your area.
- Contact ABFDE (www.abfde.org). Their Web site lists certified document examiners. E-mail one near you and see if they'll answer some questions over the phone. If they're close enough, ask if they'll meet with you.

GET AN INTERNSHIP

Look for an internship with a local law enforcement agency or a forensic laboratory.

LEARN ABOUT OTHER JOBS IN FORENSICS

- There are forensics labs in many police departments and sheriff's offices.
- You can also find out about working in the medical examiner's office.
- Or try one of these U.S. agencies: Drug Enforcement Administration (DEA); Bureau of Alcohol, Tobacco and Firearms (ATF); Federal Bureau of Investigation (FBI); United States Postal Service (USPS); Secret Service (SS); Central Intelligence Agency (CIA); the military forces; the United States Fish and Wildlife Services (FWS).

Resources

Looking for more information about handwriting analysis? Here are some resources you don't want to miss!

PROFESSIONAL ORGANIZATIONS

American Board of Forensic Document Examiners

www.abfde.org
7887 San Felipe, Suite 122
Houston, TX 77063
PHONE: 713-784-9537

The American Board of Forensic Document Examiners runs this Web site. Check out their frequently asked questions page.

American Handwriting Analysis Foundation

www.handwritingfoundation.org
P.O. Box 6201
San Jose, CA 95150-6201
PHONE: 800-826-7774

The American Handwriting Analysis Foundation is an informational resource for both experts and the general public.

Federal Bureau of Investigation (FBI)

www.fbi.gov
935 Pennsylvania Avenue, NW
Washigton, DC 20535
PHONE: 202-324-3000

The FBI has a great Web site. Check out their section for kids in grades 6-12 for real-life examples of how all the forensic investigators can work together on one case.

WEB SITES

Careers in Forensic Science

www.forensicdna.com/careers.htm

This site offers an overview of requirements and options for a forensic science career.

Court TV's Crime Library

www.crimelibrary.com

Are you curious about some of the crimes in this book? This Web site goes into them in much more detail.

Forensic Files

www.forensicfiles.com

This is the Web site for *Forensic Files* on Court TV, which features real forensic cases.

Handwriting Analysts Group

www.handwriting.org

This Web site has examples of handwriting analysis. It is a great introduction to graphology.

Louisiana Forgery/Fraud Investigators Association

www.laffia.com

The Web site gives tips to businesses and individuals on how to protect themselves from crimes of forgery and fraud.

BOOKS ABOUT THESE CASES

Fisher, Jim. *The Lindbergh Case.* Piscataway, N.J.: Rutgers University Press, 1987.

Harris, Robert. *Selling Hilter.* New York: Pantheon, 1986.

Rendell, Kenneth W. *Forging History: The Detection of Fake Letters and Documents.* Norman: University of Oklahoma Press, 1994.

BOOKS ABOUT HANDWRITING ANALYSIS

Ellen, David. *Scientific Examination of Documents.* Boca Raton, Fla.: CRC Press, 2005.

Fisher, Barry A. J. *Techniques of Crime Scene Investigation, 7th ed.* Boca Raton, Fla.: CRC Press, 2003.

Genge, Ngaire, E. *The Forensic Casebook: The Science of Crime Scene Investigation.* New York: Ballantine, 2002.

Lowe, Sheila. *The Complete Idiot's Guide to Handwriting Analysis.* New York: Alpha, 1999.

Morris, Ron N. *Forensic Handwriting Identification: Fundamental Concepts and Principles.* Burlington, Mass.: Academic Press, 2000.

BOOKS FOR KIDS ABOUT FORENSIC SCIENCE

Camenson, Blythe. *Opportunities in Forensic Science Careers.* New York: McGraw-Hill, 2001.

Platt, Richard. *Ultimate Guide to Forensic Science.* New York: DK Publishing, 2003.

Rainis, Kenneth G. *Crime-Solving Science Projects: Forensic Science Experiments.* Berkeley Heights, N.J.: Enslow Publishing, 2000.

Walker, Pam, and Elaine Wood. *Crime Scene Investigations: Real-Life Science Labs for Grades 6–12.* New York: Jossey-Bass, 1998.

A

analysis (uh-NAL-uh-siss) *noun* the process of studying something

ancestor (AN-sess-tur) *noun* a person from your family who lived a long time ago

artifact (AHR-tuh-fakt) *noun* an object someone made, usually a long time ago

B

baseline (BAYSS-line) *noun* the bottom of a line of writing

beam (beem) *noun* a long, heavy piece of wood used in constructing buildings

binocular microscope (bye-NAHK-yoo-lur MY-kroh-scope) *noun* magnifying device with lenses for both eyes

C

charity (CHAIR-uh-tee) *noun* an organization that collects money and supplies to support a particular group

CIA (SEE-eye-aye) *noun* a U.S. government organization that gathers and analyzes information about other governments. It stands for *Central Intelligence Agency*.

D

disguise (diss-GIZE) *verb* to hide your identity. In handwriting, to pretend your writing is different than it really is.

distinctly (dih-STIN-klee) *adverb* describing something that is notable or unmistakable

DNA (DEE-en-ay) *noun* a chemical found in almost every cell of your body. It's a blueprint for the way you look and function. It's short for *deoxyribonucleic acid*.

document (DOK-yoo-mehnt) *noun* a paper or collection of papers with any kind of writing on it

E

evidence (EV-uh-duhnss) *noun* information and facts that help you prove something

examiner (eg-ZAM-uhn-ur) *noun* someone who studies something closely

expert (EX-purt) *noun* someone who knows a lot about a certain subject. For a list of forensic experts, see page 12.

F

FBI (ef-BEE-eye) *noun* a U.S. government agency that investigates major crimes. It's short for *Federal Bureau of Investigation*.

forensic (fuh-REHN-zik) *adjective* describing a science that relates to the law and solving crimes

forensic document examiner (fuh-REN-zik DOK-yoo-mehnt eg-ZAM-uhn-ur) *noun* a person who uses scientific methods to find forgeries and fakes on any kind of paperwork. He or she also finds out who wrote a document if the author is not known.

forgery (FORJ–ree) *noun* an illegal copy of someone's writing. Also fake money or paintings.

fraud (frawd) *noun* a system of cheating or tricking someone

G

graphology (GRAF-ol-uh-gee) *noun* the study of handwriting to understand personality

H

handwriting analysis (HAND-rye-ting uh-NAL-uh-siss) *noun* the careful, step-by-step study of writing done by hand

I

investigation (in-VESS-tuh-gay-shun) *noun* the effort to find out as much as possible about something, such as a crime

J

jury (JU-ree) *noun* a group of people who listen to a court case and decide if someone is guilty or innocent

K

kidnapper (KID-nap-ur) *noun* a person who takes someone against his or her will and holds as prisoner, often until someone else pays for the prisoner's release

known document (nohn DOK-yoo-mehnt) *noun* a piece of writing whose author is certain. It is used for comparison with a questioned document.

L

light box (lyte box) *noun* a tool that shines light from underneath, making papers and other materials easier to see. For handwriting analysis, it helps examiners notice evidence of tracing.

P

pound (pound) *noun* a unit of money in Great Britain

pressure (PRESH-ur) *noun* how hard the writer presses on a pen or pencil

protractor (proh-TRAK-tur) *noun* a tool used for measuring and drawing angles

Q

questioned document (KWES-chund DOK-yoo-mehnt) *noun* a piece of writing that is studied and compared to a known document

R

ransom (RAN-suhm) *noun* money demanded in exchange for releasing someone held captive

S

scam (skam) *noun* a trick, usually as a way to get money

Secret Service (SEE-krit SUR-vuss) *noun* a U.S. government group that protects the U.S. President and works to prevent counterfeit (fake) money

serial number (SEER-ee-ul NUM-bur) *noun* a series of numbers, and sometimes letters, that identifies an item

signature (SIG-nuh-chur) *noun* the special way that you sign your name, usually in cursive

slant (slant) *verb* to be at an angle

statistic (stuh-TISS-tik) *noun* a fact expressed as a number or percentage

suspect (SUS-pekt) *noun* a person law enforcement officials think might be guilty of a crime

W

will (wil) *noun* written instructions about who should receive the property of someone who dies

Index

Photo Credits: Photographs © 2007: Alamy Images/Popperfoto: 35; AP/Wide World Photos: 64; Corbis Images: 5 top, 15, 16, 18, 19, 21, 23, 24, 25, 44 right (Bettmann), 27 (Jason Hawkes), 10 left (Library of Congress), 14 bottom, 46 right (Matthew Polak/Sygma), cover, 32 (Royalty-Free), 38 (Michel Ulli/Reuters); Dr. Fausto Brugnatelli: 46 left; Everett Collection, Inc./CBS: 6, 47; Getty Images: 30 (James Baigrie), 5 center (Ron Chapple), 48 bottom right (Dorling Kindersley), 56 (John Foxx), 48 top right (Laurent Hamels), 5 bottom, 37 (Keystone), 49 center (Dave King), 42 top (Matthew Klein), 45 (Ben Martin), 49 top (Photodisc), 14 top (Spencer Rowell/VCL), 39 bottom (Michael Urban); Glenbridge Publishing Ltd.: 11 top, 33, 44 left (from *Great Forgers and Famous Fakes*); Grant R. Sperry: 52; Index Stock Imagery/Hoa Qui: 4 bottom, 8; Collection of Kenneth W. Rendell: 41, 42 center, 42 bottom; Mark Walch/B. Brouse: 26; Mike Gunnill: 29, 34; NEWSCOM: 40 (Ingo Roehrbein/AFP), 39 top (Michael Urban/AFP); Ron Kimball Stock: 31; Sirchie Fingerprint Laboratories: 1, 54; Reprinted by permission of the University of Oklahoma Press, Norman: 4 top, 10 right, 11 bottom (from *Forging History: The Detection of Fake Letters and Documents*, by Kenneth Rendell); VEER: 49 bottom (Photodisc Photography), 48 left (Stockbyte Photography). Maps by David Lindroth, Inc.

Author's Note

I'm a writer. I'm not a handwriting analyst. But one of the great things about being a writer is all the new things you get to learn.

I did research for this book at the library, on the Internet, and—the most fun—by talking with people who are forensic document examiners and graphologists. They all are passionate about their jobs. And they're eager to have young people study their profession.

One of my challenges was researching the Lindbergh kidnapping. More than 100 books have been written about Charles Lindbergh and this case. (If you don't believe me, search on amazon.com for "Lindbergh.") I had to narrow my focus. I went to the source that several other sources quoted. Jim Fisher's book, *The Lindbergh Case*, is well researched and well written. It really captured the drama of the case, and how the whole world was watching it.

CONTENT ADVISER: Andre A. Moenssens, Douglas Stripp Professor of Law Emeritus, University of Missouri at Kansas City, Forensic Consultant

[Forensic Fact]

DID YOU KNOW that January 23 is National Handwriting Day? It's also John Hancock's birthday! (He's the famous founding father with the BIGGEST signature on the Declaration of Independence.)